LAWYER UP!

BRUCE DENSON

Lawyer Up!
Work Smarter, Dress Sharper, & Bring Your
A-Game To Court (And Life)

by Bruce Denson

Printed in the United States of America

www.thedensonfirm.com

Published by T&G Press

DEDICATION

This book is dedicated to the two groups of lawyers that have pushed me to become more professional. Thank you to those attorneys that have led by good example. And I am grateful for those that have otherwise inspired me, as well.

SUMMARY OF CONTENTS

CONTENTS

ABOUT THIS BOOK

This book is broken down into three sections – Inside, Outside, and What Not To Wear To Court. The sections are intended to be practical, inspirational, and humorous in turn.

The first section, Inside, is about getting your mind right and your head in the game. It's a distillation of practical tips for lawyers to maximize their day-to-day work and tackle their long-term career goals. The five chapters of Section I break down the essential elements of a professional practice and healthy work/life balance. Additionally, each section is followed by at least one Sidebar with some practice pointers to achieve these bigger goals.

The second section, Outside, is the summary of research into how what we wear influences others and ourselves. As advocates for our clients, it is our duty to take advantage of every opportunity to present their position in the best light possible. As demonstrated by science, what we wear has an impact on judges, juries, opposing counsel, and ourselves.

The final section, What Not To Wear To Court, stands in contrast to the first two sections. It's a gallery of pictures I've taken at Florida courthouses over the last few years. While it's included to provide some comic relief, it's not intended to ridicule anybody. Rather, my intention here is to emphasize that what we wear to court can literally speak volumes; be sure your clients are sending the right message.

SECTION I:
INSIDE

▮ INTRODUCTION

Being professional is a long game. But it's an attitude, presence and stature formed in the short term – by our daily decisions and actions. The benefits of being professional accrue over time. Those benefits are paid for by our everyday work and require patience.

Sometimes shortcuts appear tempting. The easy way out on a case may hold allure. So it's important to look at the long term and focus on professionalism. What may appear expeditious in the short run often has a negative impact on your career.

Being seen by your peers and your community as a professional doesn't happen overnight. Even with a firm commitment to your ideals it takes years to build a rock-solid reputation. And there is no specific tipping point when the "status" of professional is conveyed, there is no ceremony.

Once established, it requires ongoing maintenance. But the good news is that once it's established, it also tends to perpetuate itself to some degree.

But not if you aren't careful. Professional reputations can vanish in an instant, with a single bad decision. However, the more you focus on professionalism, the less likely you are to make those bad decisions. Of course we all make mistakes. Fortunately, the more time, energy and focus you've invested in professionalism, the more likely a mistake will be forgiven.

The idea of this book is simply to give you a moment to think about professionalism and the benefits it can have on your career. The five short chapters are written to provide you with actionable items as well. Professionalism manifests in action, not just thought. My hope is that this book inspires you to take a look at your day-to-day habits and find improvement. I hope that you look at your career and create a path to happiness. And I also hope that you look at your legal community – and by extension the world around you - and find a way to make it better.

Chapter 1

PREPARE

A lawyer should be fully prepared when appearing
at court or in hearings.

- Professionalism Expectations 4.13

P reparation, the keystone of professionalism, is so vitally important to each and every case that you almost can't do enough of it. It is the biggest chapter in this book for a reason.

No matter what else you do, if you don't prepare, you will never be the professional you want to be, and you will never be comfortable in the courtroom. Planning well at the beginning will eliminate problems at the end. Have I got your attention? Good. This is crucial. But at the same time, I don't want you to get stuck in the preparation stage, driving both yourself and your client crazy with endless minutia.

The following 10 "Preparation Points" checklist, compiled after years in the legal trenches, will ensure you do just the right amount of prep work to get your case off to a solid start.

1. KNOW THE FACTS & CLIENT EARLY

Five minutes ago, you were perfect strangers. Now this person sitting in front of you is putting his very future in your hands.

Daunting? Without a doubt – especially for a new lawyer.

Still, it's Job One to get to know your client and his case inside-out, up and down, backward and forward. So shelve those jitters for the moment and let's get moving.

While it's your prerogative to wait until after the first client meeting to do any case recon, I usually like to spend at least an hour familiarizing myself with anything I can get my hands on. This can mean trying to find out, at the very least:
- Whether the client has any litigation history
- Whether there's been any publicity around this particular case
- Whether there are any precedents set that we can use as a jumping-off point

By gathering this type of data in advance, I'm then able to customize what I like to call my "Opening Spiel." If that sounds glib, or jokey, trust that it isn't; I couldn't be more serious about the task at hand, which is to set my client's mind at ease.

Included in my opener is the previous experience I've had in handling similar cases, and a top-lining of the process, and steps, my client can expect as his own case unfolds.

For criminal and more complicated civil cases, I go more in-depth about the process. Sometimes I'll even use an actual flow-chart to map-out the stages. Though this detailed type of road-map can sometimes make the client a bit nervous, I feel it's necessary. In the courtroom, unlike at birthday parties, surprises are to be avoided at all costs.

My other agenda in speaking first is to build trust. I often tell my clients that seeing an attorney is like seeing a doctor. Not only do they need to feel confident enough to share details, it's critically *important* that they do. I need to know where it hurts so I know where to operate. There's no way I can do the best job possible for them if I don't know everything. And I assure them that attorney-client privilege makes my office – or anywhere we privately interact – an absolute safe haven for full disclosure.

Next it's time for my client to speak. If they're on edge about doing so, I usually get the ball rolling by trying to elicit their top concerns. If it's a criminal case, that might be: "I don't want to go to jail." If it's a DUI, it's probably: "I don't want to lose my license." If it is a civil case, I like to start with what the client hopes to accomplish.

While your client is talking, be sure to take copious notes. No matter how great you think your memory is, don't rely on it – ever. Notes are especially important in a criminal case, because you'll undoubtedly be faced with closing the gap between what your *client* says happened and what the *State* says happened.

For civil cases, and personal injury, this first client meeting is more about collecting the 5 Ws: Who, What, Where, When and Why. Still, I urge you to take notes. Often I will give the client a copy of the notes, for them to review to make sure I got a clear understanding of what they told me.

With that first meeting under your belt, and your budding relationship with your new client on firm footing, it's time for Step 2.

2. KNOW THE BURDEN

At the risk of sounding very Law School 101, the burden of proof is the duty placed upon a party to prove or disprove a disputed fact or claim. It also defines which party bears the burden. In a criminal case, the State shoulders the burden to demonstrate that the defendant is guilty. In a civil case, the plaintiff normally carries the burden of proof. However, in criminal and civil cases the defendant may carry a burden if certain defenses are asserted.

The burden of proof also encapsulates the burden of persuasion, or the amount of proof a party with the burden must establish. There is a big difference in proving a case beyond a reasonable doubt and proving a case by a preponderance of the evidence.

At the beginning of your preparation it is crucial to know who has the burden and to what extent must they carry it.

In simple terms, the party bringing charges typically bears the primary responsibility for proving its case. In criminal cases, the party without the burden of proof is shielded under the presumption of innocence. In civil cases, the burden is initially on the plaintiff. However, in some instances – primarily in *"prima facie"* cases – the burden can shift to the defendant.

Get clear on the full extent of the burden, and the role – if any - your client will play in carrying it.

3. RESEARCH THE LAW

You could – and should – spend a good chunk of time researching the law specific to your case. Still, there's a way to work *smarter* rather than harder at this stage. And if you can put together a reliable list of resources and high-quality shortcuts to help you gather information quickly, that will ultimately prove extremely valuable to both your overall efficiency and balance.

In Florida, where I practice, I've got my short list of trusty "Go To" resources, including:

• **Erhardt's Florida Evidence:** Compiled by Professor Charles W. Ehrhardt, a former federal prosecutor, and first published in 1984, this is a review of every new Florida and federal case that involves evidence. It's updated annually, and while pricey – in the ballpark of $500 – I've found it well worth the cost. To save money, you might consider subscribing to a monthly service that includes all updates. For more information, go to <u>legalsolutions.thomsonreuters.com</u>.

- **Florida Jurisprudence, 2d (aka Fla Jur) for your practice area:** You can purchase all 400 volumes for about $17,000, but you probably just need your practice area to drill down to the material you need in your area of focus.

4. KNOW THE JUDGE

As a fresh-from-law-school attorney, you might be thinking: *How am I supposed to do that?*

If you're employed by a firm, you're in luck; most of the seasoned lawyers around you will be happy to fill you in on Judge So-And-So's pet peeves and idiosyncrasies. Maybe Judge So-And-So doesn't like the sound of briefcases with snapping locks, or striped blue ties, or the word "thereabout" – it could be anything. The more quirks and potential landmines you can uncover, the better; it's all about controlling the variables.

For those of you in solo practice, I highly encourage you to be pro-active. Dive in and join every local legal organization you can. Get out and mingle, network and make connections. It's every bit as important to your career as buckling down with those books.

My local bar association, for example, organizes a lunch at least six times a year that allows us to interact with judges in our district. There's also a judicial reception every year.

It's smart to try to research your local judges online, too. Every judicial circuit has a website where you can compile, at the very least, names and basic info about each judge. From there, you can widen your search via the Internet.

While on the judicial circuit website, you may also come across other stray tidbits that could come in handy in the future. As I was writing this section, I hopped on the site for my local district – the Sixth Judicial Circuit, serving Pasco and Pinellas Counties in Florida. There, in the "news" section, I saw that one of the judges had finished in the top five of a recent Ironman competition. Should I happen to run into this same judge at the next St. Pete or Clearwater Bar lunch, I'll have something to chat about.

No, I'm not suggesting you become a world-class schmoozer. But having a topic at hand when the opportunity for small-talk presents itself is just smart business. And learning a little about the judges who hear your cases can give you a decided edge over the competition.

Which brings me to the next step…

5. KNOW THE OPPOSING COUNSEL

Because of the nature of the work I do, I tend to see the same attorneys over and over – and that's especially true for the criminal cases. Luckily, my fellow defense attorneys and I all get along pretty well. In general, it's a friendly bunch. Not only are we running into each other in court a lot, there's also a well-trafficked cafeteria at the county courthouse that brings us into each other's orbits on a regular basis.

On the civil side of the fence, I'll admit that it isn't quite as convivial. Particularly with some of the tobacco cases I've taken on that have pitted me, a solo practitioner, against armies of litigators with deep corporate pockets at their disposal.

If you're new on the scene, you obviously haven't come in much contact with opposing counsel yet. So you'll need to do your homework. And this is again where networking – and becoming a member of your local bar association - will come in handy. And don't just join – participate. If they're organizing a golf outing, by all means go. Not into sports? Swing by the monthly happy hour and have a beer. Or sign up for a Continuing Legal Ed class. Just do it. Show up. See and be seen.

The benefits of building at least a semblance of a relationship with opposing counsel are myriad. But let's start with the most important one – ease in reaching agreements – which just happens to be the subject of my next Preparation Point.

6. CONFER WITH OPPOSING COUNSEL

It's the rare case that actually goes to trial these days. And that means one thing: Both sides have to work together to iron out their differences and come to an agreement. Solid communication that moves a case to resolution isn't just a good idea, it's an obligation.
A judge hearing your case wants to know that both sides have tried – hard - to resolve issues before they step one foot in his courtroom. Federal court and most local jurisdictions require the attorneys confer before bringing a matter before the court.

To ensure maximum efficiency, strive for excellent communication with opposing counsel before meeting with the judge. Once you're engaged in the heat of battle, you're sure to have plenty of opportunities to toughen your stance.

7. DRAFT A PROPOSED ORDER

As you begin preparing for a hearing, start with drafting a proposed order.

Given that a proposed order is essentially a best-case-scenario "wish list" of

everything you'd like the judge to order at the *end* of the case, it may seem counter-intuitive - or at the very least premature - to draft it at the beginning,
I recommend doing so anyway. Starting with the end in mind can really bring clarity to your thinking and preparation around a case, and ensure that you won't leave out any vitally important detail. It's one more way you're going above and beyond the call of duty for your client, and laying the groundwork for a positive outcome.

8. OUTLINE YOUR POSITION

Time has flown, your research and preparation to this point is virtually bulletproof and your court date - and face-to-face encounter with the judge - is imminent. Now is most definitely not the time to drop the ball with a shoddy, rambling, disorganized argument.

Obviously you won't be *reading* to the judge, but you can certainly refer to a detailed outline that covers every major point you need to make. The physical format –notes on a legal pad, a Word doc - is up to you. Just be sure to triple-check it so it's flawless.

Then take it a step further and outline your opponent's argument, too. Put yourself in opposing counsel's shoes and try to decode the way his mental wheels are turning. What would *you* be presenting if you were on the other side? Again, surprises are the enemy, so pick them off early and often.

9. PLAN FOR AN APPEAL

It happens - things don't go your client's way in court.

There's a way to mitigate the fall-out, but bear with me - it sounds like a real downer of a strategy: Before you even show up for that first hearing, imagine that you've already lost.

Yes, this is my tip: Imagine that you've already lost. No matter how convinced you are of the solidity of your case, envision the opposite of the result you're expecting – a loss.

Why is this helpful? Because on appeal, you're strictly confined to whatever has been previously presented; not a single shred of new evidence can surface.

That's why you need to work backward and be 1000 percent sure that you're admitting everything into the record that needs to be there in the event of an appeal.

I can assure you there's nothing more painful than looking in the rearview mirror and spotting a case-making piece of evidence or argument that you neglected to include. So go negative to achieve a positive outcome. That's what winning lawyers do.

10. RELAX

Prepare. Then, relax and execute.

Yes, relax. When you're calm, you perform to the utmost of your abilities. Or, as Bill Murray says, "No matter what it is, no matter what your job is, the more relaxed you are, the better you are." I'm with Bill on this one.

■ SIDEBARS

FINDING A MENTOR

In every city, in each area of practice, there are inevitably one or two lawyers who are the "go-to" attorneys. They've been in practice a long time. They've established themselves to be knowledgeable in the their field. They have an iron-clad reputation for professionalism.

You will likely find that attorneys of this caliber are more than happy to have coffee or lunch with you. It never hurts to ask, and it's nice to have a relationship with attorneys who have a breadth of experience that you haven't yet acquired.

It takes a little courage to cold-call (or, more likely, cold-email) a more seasoned attorney, but I know you've got it in you to build these all-important career contacts.

If you need some direction, the Young Lawyers Division of the Florida Bar can get you pointed the right way. They have <u>a list</u> of mentoring programs throughout the state.

EDC FOR LAWYERS

Survivalists have with them at all times a group of items called EDC, short for Every Day Carry. This is a small list of things needed to deal with everyday life, and possible emergency situations. For survivalists EDC usually includes pocketknives, firestarters and other tools that wouldn't make it past the deputies at the courthouse. But lawyers also should have a stocked EDC list in their briefcase or case bag. I always carry the following to the courthouse-2 pens, highlighter, legal pad, Post it notes, USB drive, reading glasses, and because it is Florida — a pocket umbrella.

The idea is to have the tools you need for the circumstances you may be facing. Obviously, this list grows when headed to the courthouse for trial or extended hearings. Your list may vary.

Chapter 2 —————————————————————

KEEP YOUR EYE ON THE HORIZON

A lawyer must routinely keep clients informed and attempt to resolve client concerns.

- Professionalism Expectations 1.11

D o you plan on being a lawyer for a long time? The clients you work with down the road are a direct result of the effort you put in today. Careers are a slow build. The quality of the clients and cases you work on in 5 to 10 years are a direct result of the quality of work you do now. Clients, colleagues and judges talk. Word gets around. The cream rises to the top. Good lawyering begets good cases. Make the most of your current opportunities.

Start each case with a goal – avoid conviction, recover losses, prove no negligence, etc. – and the end in mind. One easy and very effective way to firm up your thinking around goals and the end-game you're hoping to achieve is to write a letter to your client at the very beginning of representation. While that may sound overly formal, it's actually incredibly helpful for everyone involved. Your client's goal should be clearly stated and attainable. It is the duty of the lawyer to be informed about all forms of resolution and to counsel clients accordingly.

Case goals are measured against the facts and the law in order to determine just how much relief we can realistically achieve. Each goal will have its own set of public and private burdens, and you'll need to walk your client through all of that. Goals can be audacious and aggressive, but those come with a higher cost and greater uncertainty. Remember: Surprises are the enemy; always err on the side of information overload.

In law, as in life, there are ramifications for every decision. Your job as an attorney is to make *very* sure that your client understands the pros and cons – and potential impact – of choosing A over B. You should counsel a client about the pluses and minuses of pursuing their claims as compared with the benefits to be achieved.
To do that, you'll need to not only know your own particular case inside-out and the general laws pertaining to it, but also the full range of options and outcomes. Some clients will need to be talked back from their BHAG (Big Hairy Audacious Goal) and others will need to encouraged that they can be more aggressive in their approach. Only once there is a clear objective and timeframe can the work begin.

When it comes to goals I like referring to the SMART acronym coined by George Doran. Ideally speaking, case goals should be:

·   *Specific* – target a specific outcome.

·   *Measurable* – be able to gauge progress.

·   *Assignable* – specify who will handle which parts of the case.

·   *Realistic* – state what results can realistically be achieved, given the facts and law.

·   *Timeframe* – specify how quickly the case can be resolved.

In formulating your SMART goals it is helpful to have excellent persuasion skills. I guarantee there will be times when you strongly recommend one course of action over the other, and clients don't always have the right instincts, or act in their own best interests. Help them do that by nudging them in the opposite direction when you know they're headed down the wrong path. (And when you can't convince them, do a CYA letter!)

Setting a timeframe for closing cases is crucial. Setting a goal of how and when a case should be resolved and then working toward that goal saves time, money and stress for clients and for attorneys. Make sure your client understands the timeframe needed for the resolution they seek and keep them updated on any events that change that timeframe.

In the long run, you will prosper more if you avoid creating or extending litigation. Winning at all costs will close more doors than it will open. It is more important to establish yourself as a lawyer people can trust to resolve their issues.

A practice built on selfishness and a no-holds-barred mentality cannot be sustained and is shortsighted. A lawyer's reputation as a problem solver will result in happier clients and a prosperous life.

■ SIDEBARS

SETTING CAREER GOALS

Your clients are Priority One. But right on the heels of that — Priority Two — is keeping your career on an upward trajectory. Attorneys that have career goals are most likely to have a career that grows.

Patience is key here. While some weeks, months - even years — might leave you feeling like you're in a bit of a holding pattern, trust that if you persevere, you'll get where you want to go, career-wise.

As always, start with a roadmap. Write down a detailed plan that includes not only your goals (the more specific the better), but also the steps you'll need to achieve them. Moving forward, those steps will serve as an action plan to steer you closer to your desired endpoint. Do you need to take a Continuing Ed class? Confer with your mentor? Dive into extra research? Breaking down large goals into smaller tasks makes them easier to facilitate.

Lastly, but perhaps most importantly, attach a time-frame to each goal. This is crucial. While it doesn't have to be written in stone, you're much more likely to achieve a goal with a date attached to it than one that falls into the "some day" category. No one graduates law school — or wins cases - by falling into the "some day" trap. Now that you're a practicing attorney, let's keep that momentum going.

MANAGING CLIENT EXPECTATIONS

Clients rely heavily on our advice and they set their expectations based on what their attorney tells them. That's why it's important to build trust from the get-go, whether it's a quick initial phone chat to a more formal, in-office consult.

Never promise a client more than you can deliver. Bar rules prohibit you from guaranteeing a particular result, so make it clear that you are not making any promises other than to give the case your best efforts.

Make it a practice to under-promise and over-deliver. Set realistic expectations at the first meeting. Never make a promise you cannot keep just to sign up a case.

Occasionally, a client will tell me that they met with another attorney who promised them a particular result. I always tell them that if they are comfortable with that attorney, they should get that promise in writing and hire them. More often than not, they come back and hire me.

Chapter 3

MOVE FORWARD WITH CONFIDENCE

A lawyer must not engage in dilatory or delay tactics.

- Professionalism Expectations 4.6

Like riding a bike, it's easier to be professional if you're moving your cases forward. Stalled cases are good for no one. Judges get aggravated, Plaintiff lawyers aren't getting paid, and no defense lawyer wants to gain a reputation as a person who in bad faith grinds cases to a halt. Criminal defendants don't want charges perpetually hanging overhead, especially given the fact that living with that kind of stress can generate poor decisions in other areas of their lives. And State Attorneys don't want evidence or witnesses to disappear, a distinct possibility if a case kicks around too long.

If you find yourself waking up at four in the morning stressed about work that anxiety is probably due to two things. One, you are not moving your case forward when it needs to be. Or two, the case is moving forward and you have delayed in your plans to deal with that forward movement. Confidence (and sleep) comes with forward movement.

Develop within yourself an urgency for closure. To do that, you'll have to learn how to be realistic about the actual progress you're making. Merely being busy is not progress. Seek efficiency in forward movement by getting in the habit of asking yourself one key question:

"What can I do next to advance this case toward closure?"

If whatever task you're currently engaged in isn't delivering forward momentum for your case, it's likely a waste of time. Move on. Or, at the very least, put it on the back burner. Don't confuse activity with progress.

Remember, hope is not a legal strategy and wishing is not a valid legal position. You must put in the work and take action on your cases. The Ready-Fire-Aim approach does not work for lawyers! Fire with assured precision after you put in the work. Prioritize your SMART goals and move forward knowing that you are not going to shoot your client in the foot.

Here's a tip I wish I'd been given when I was starting out: Use forms and checklists for cases judiciously. There is no need to reinvent every wheel. Legal forms and templates are a good place to start, but tailor your approach to each case. There are no magic formulas that work in all cases. Through experience you will develop pleadings and techniques helpful to your practice. Keep a "Form File" to use as a starting point for the next case, but always keep in mind it is just the starting point and considerations of the current case and changes in the law must be made before going to the courthouse. Check with other practitioners in your practice area which Form Books/Sites they find most useful.

While I understand the desire to wait until you're "totally" ready before stepping into court, I'll let you in on a secret: You may *never* feel that way. Most lawyers *always* think there's more work that could be done.

The law tends to attract people who like to dot every i and cross every t, but that's nearly impossible – if you want to eventually move on and land new clients, that is!

Your mission is to override your doubts about your preparation, and possible concerns about whether the other side has a better grip on the case than you do. You need to move forward regardless. Work hard and be confident in your preparation. You owe that to your client. Remember: They've placed their trust and faith in you; now's the time to show them they've made the right choice.

Learn to trust that you'll be able to meet the challenges, and potential setbacks, that surface in your case as you're going along. If you've incorporated the core principles of Part II – *Keep Your Eye On the Horizon* – you'll already be in "anticipation mode" and disciplining yourself to prepare contingency plans on a continual basis.

Rock-solid confidence in yourself will only come with time. But trust me, you'll get there. And true to Newton's First Law of Motion, once your career has forward momentum, that confidence will tend to maintain your trajectory.

■ SIDEBARS ──────────────────────

KEEP AN "ACTION" LIST

Whenever I start to feel stressed in my practice, it is usually because I have gotten away from my Action List. I have found one of the most effective ways to bring my stress level down is to go through my files and rewrite my Action List. This ensures I have touched all my files, I know what needs to be done next and I can spread these tasks over my calendar.

Need some help getting started, you might want to check out The Checklist Manifesto, by Atul Gawande, for the why and how of making a checklist work for you. As the complexity of our profession increases an Action list becomes more valuable to make sure your cases get handled properly.

The purpose of an Action List — whatever format you eventually land on and feel comfortable with — is threefold:
1. It helps you determine which delaying tactics are legit and which aren't
2. It serves as a handy To Do list of pending matters
3. It moves the case forward

So what goes on your Action List? Every pending matter, which will be reviewed - at the very least - on a monthly basis. Make note of the last action taken on it, as well as the date. Keep shuffling the items so that a matter that has had no recent activity gets moved to the top. By activity, I mean both small stuff (telephone calls, email) and large (complaint filing, a settlement, or possible move for dismissal). The big idea behind an Action list is to act.

I am not a big fan of the "Honey Do" list at home. But the reality is life can get busy and the office isn't the only place where things need to get done. Just like the office, an Action List can help you prioritize, schedule and accomplish things on the homefront.

DON'T DELAY

Stalling for time is a common legal strategy, and it's tied to the notion that if you wait long enough, or throw a big enough blizzard of paperwork at a case, the other side will eventually pack up and go home. But know this: You can and will be disciplined if your delaying tactics are found to have no merit.

The Florida Bar recommends asking yourself whether an independent, competent attorney, one who is acting in good faith, would view the specific action you're thinking of taking as actually necessary and not merely a delaying tactic. If not, don't pursue it. See Comment to Rule 4-3.2, Florida Rules of Professional Conduct.

A reputation as a problem-solver, rather than a problem-creator, will advance your career. A reputation as an attorney that grinds cases to a halt, may have the same affect on your practice.

ARRIVE EARLY TO THE COURTHOUSE

You can eliminate the majority of problems (and resulting stressors) in your practice by focusing on two things: being prepared on the issues and being on time. Having a reputation for timeliness and preparation can do a lot of the work for you.

Let's start with the easiest piece of this puzzle: punctuality.

If you're walking into a courtroom or judge's chambers for a hearing at the designated start time, you're late.

Ten minutes early? That's on time. Better yet, make it 15.

Being late to a hearing is not only rude, it immediately puts you at a disadvantage

—for two very important reasons. One, you'll make a bad impression on the judge hearing your case, and that's **never** a sound strategy. And two, if you're rushing to get to the courtroom you're going to race through your opening argument and you're far more likely to forget something important.

That's why the expression "you never get a second chance to make a first impression" is more applicable in a court of law than just about anywhere else.

You've put in so many hours of prep work, why would you risk not being able to showcase that effort? And more crucially, why would you jeopardize your client's future by not getting off on the right foot with the judge who has the power to make or break your case?

I've seen cases go off the rails from the get-go because an attorney didn't give himself enough time to collect his thoughts before launching into his opening argument.

And unfortunately, that can trigger a domino effect.

Lawyers are expected to be prepared to respond to issues very quickly. The amount of preparation required is driven by two main factors: chaos in the environment and the time allowed for response. Law offices and trials can be extremely chaotic environments that require immediate responses. Offices and courtrooms have chaotic flare-ups because the vast majority of chaos is caused by humans, and humans (clients, attorneys, witnesses, judges, jurors, etc.) are quite unpredictable. Taking steps in advance to reduce chaos and establishing protocols to deal with surprises are key to preparation.

By showing up on time, you've already reduced a fair amount of chaos. And guess who else needs to be punctual? Your client. This is critical, so ensure it happens by doing a "test-run" first. Take your client to the courthouse, show him where to park, walk him right into the courtroom. (If you don't already know where your judge hangs his hat, you can find out on the judicial circuit website I recommended you visit way back in Preparation Point 4, "Know the Judge.")

Then it's time to plan for all known contingencies. Think through and plan for each finite range of outcomes. Second, have a basic response framework for unexpected surprises outside of that range. Lawyers, like pilots, should have checklists to work through when encountering unexpected challenges. Because of the chaos inherent in the profession it is essential to have checklists and a general-purpose framework to work through unexpected issues.

Take a monthly look at:

A. ***Your balance of work and social/family, spiritual life and fitness.*** (I know you don't have time to do 50 crunches, but you need to. Also: Call your mom and go to church.)

B. ***Your case load.*** In short, keep it reasonable. I'll discuss ways to do that in a bit.

C. ***Your ratio of working hard to playing hard.*** Make sure neither is getting out of whack.

D. ***Your resources budget.*** Fairly anticipated time and resources required for both individual tasks and big-picture projects. Refer back to *Professionalism Expectations 1.4* regularly, and be sure you're not over-promising and under-delivering. Not only is that a bad business practice, it's also a recipe for stress.

I realize I've just thrown a lot at you – another To Do list on top of the one you already have. To get you started, here are a few handy thoughts to consider and steps to take:

IDEAS TO WEIGH:

1. **Ask:** What is out of balance in your life?

2. **Identify:** What is the one thing you can do each day or each week to help you create balance?

3. **Assess:** How do you measure balance in your life? Do you have goals you evaluate balance against?

Before I wrap up this section with a call to philanthropy and giving back (yes, it's another add-on to your To Do list, and yes, it will help you stay balanced), I want to leave you with what I consider our profession's biggest possible sin and virtue.

The deadly sin?

Gluttony.

Too many cases, too much work, too much of anything can lead to problems. Gluttony is an impediment to balance.

The virtue to cultivate?

Moderation.

For a deeper dive into moderation, let's refer back to Section 6 of *Professionalism Expectations*: Respect for the Time and Commitments of Others. This section advises lawyers to not impose unreasonable deadlines on others (6.1), accede to reasonable requests for scheduling (6.5), and provide other affected persons ample advance notice of hearings and proceedings (6.3).

These directives can be inverted and applied to ourselves in order to create balance. Don't impose unreasonable deadlines on yourself. Keep your schedule reasonable and manageable. Give yourself time to prepare. Not only should you "[r]espect the time and commitment of others . . ." but respect your own time and commitments and lead a balanced life.

■ SIDEBARS ——————————————

PRIORITIZE PRO BONO

Balance in your practice requires pro bono work — it's that simple. Although balance is usually presented to attorneys in terms of managing their time outside of the office, the reality is, it's the office life itself - the time spent at work - that's out of balance. You will personally benefit from extending yourself, and the profession will also benefit. Pro bono will increase your sense of job satisfaction. There's no excuse not to do it.

I used to say, "I'm a criminal defense lawyer, the Public Defender handles all the pro bono cases." But that changed when I looked a little deeper and reached out to The Florida Counsel for Compulsive Gambling and requested that if they had a client with criminal problems related to gambling, to let me know.
The only way you're going to have sense of fulfillment as a person is through giving, and as an attorney, that's through pro bono.

To get you motivated, I've collected a few quotes
I find inspirational:

> **"The best way to find yourself is to lose yourself
> in the service of others." — Gandhi**

And here's what Richard Branson, founder of Virgin Airlines had to say about volunteering:

"This isn't an area where you can just go charging in, however. It is imperative that the project you propose be deeply linked to your business's mission and the sense of purpose that carries your employees through the workday.

If you are unsure about what your business's purpose is, except perhaps to make money, it might be a good time to rethink your approach. Companies that survive and thrive over the long term have more significant interactions with their customers than just conducting transactions; great businesses are places where problems are solved and lives are improved. A sense of mission helps such enterprises to keep sight of the bigger picture."

Gandhi and Richard Branson – two wildly different men with very similar core notions about the importance of giving back.

JOIN THE LOCAL BAR ASSOCIATION

There are two groups you should join. One, your local Bar association. It is important to interact with other lawyers in the community. Being a member of the local Bar will help you stay balanced throughout your career on many levels.

And two, a group that has no lawyers in it. Because if you just hang out with lawyers all the time you can become a little weird. There is certainly a group that engages in a sport or hobby that you enjoy. Relationships make our life richer, and the more diverse those people, the fuller our life becomes.

Chapter 5 —————————————————————

LEARN TO LOVE SETBACKS

A lawyer should be civil and courteous in all situations,
both professional and personal, and avoid conduct
that is degrading to the legal profession.

- Professionalism Expectations 5.2

As adults, we hopefully all accept the big picture that humans are fallible, that we aren't "perfect" 24/7, year after year. Still, we hate to apply that notion to ourselves in the present tense. We're taught that the way to succeed in life – and in the practice of law – is to never make a mistake and to never lose. That isn't even remotely realistic; not every trip to the courthouse will end successfully.

Sometimes you will take on cases with bad facts. The cards are stacked against you. Usually in those cases the outcome is adverse to your client. If you brought in a dog, you have to walk it. Don't take it too hard. Cut yourself some slack.

Likewise, sometimes you get great cases. All the evidence and witnesses line up in your favor and victory is had. Don't gloat. Don't take all the credit.

Don't judge your effort by your results. Good facts or bad facts, rest easy at the end of each day knowing you gave the case your all.

Instead of striving for perfection – an unobtainable goal - aim for excellence in the moment.

Here's a handy 5-point plan for ensuring you're doing exactly that:

1. **Know that you will not win every hearing or every trial.** By walking into the courtroom armed with that mindset, you'll stay positive and upbeat.

2. **Have backup systems ready to go.** Glitches happen. But being able to swiftly pivot to either old-school pen and paper, or even another electronic device, can save the day. The saying is, "Two is one, and one is none." Have redundant capabilities, not just redundant equipment.

3. **Be prepared with a solid contingency plan.** Need a refresher course in how to make that happen? Refer back to the ***Part II: Keep Your Eye On the Horizon*** section of this book.

4. **Don't make faces, roll eyes or continue to argue.** If you've been professional throughout, you'll have already made your best argument. Although it can be tough to do, respect the ruling and move on. (This is serious; below, in the section "Conduct Unbecoming," I've included three sections of *Professionalism Expectations* pertaining specifically to courtroom conduct in the face of defeat.)

5. **Regroup and re-motivate yourself if you don't get the outcome you're expecting.** How? By realizing that there's no shame in failing, but rather in failing to get back up. Keep at it. Present your case professionally, and don't stop doing what you know is right.

About that last point – regrouping and re-motivating - I just want you to know that I'm aware how difficult that can be. Especially when you've logged countless hours prepping a case, and really poured your heart and soul into it. I have usually convinced myself I am going to win when I walk into the courtroom. Losses are tough.

Here's something else that can crop up in our profession that you might be unaware of: compassion fatigue. Let's acknowledge, right now, that each and every one of us is at risk for that. Listening to our clients' often traumatic tales, and empathizing with them, can definitely take its toll after a while.

I recommend finding a way to actively debrief the traumatic material in your practice, perhaps by talking to colleagues about it. And definitely take a look at how balanced your life is, the topic of *Part IV* of this book. Evaluate what's causing you tension in your practice and take steps to defuse it.

What specifically drives us, and continually moves us forward despite setbacks, is different for everyone. But professionalism is inspired by getting up again and again. To achieve the resiliency to do that, it's helpful to ask yourself:

1. When is the last time you "fell off" and how did you react?
2. What gets you up and going?

CONDUCT UNBECOMING

As mentioned above, here are three *Professionalism Expectations* to bear in mind:

5.1 A lawyer should abstain from rude, disruptive, and disrespectful behavior. The lawyer should encourage clients and support personnel to do the same.

5.2 A lawyer should be civil and courteous in all situations, both professional and personal, and avoid conduct that is degrading to the legal profession. (See R. Regulating Fla. Bar 3-4.3)

5.7 A lawyer should inform clients and witnesses that approving and disapproving gestures, facial expressions, or audible comments are absolutely prohibited in legal proceedings.

■ SIDEBARS ──────────────

AVOIDING & DEALING WITH SUBSTANCE ABUSE

There's no sugar-coating the fact that we've picked a stressful profession. And unfortunately, some of us highly fallible human beings sometimes turn to drugs or alcohol to try to cope with the stress we're battling on an almost daily basis. If that's the case for you or any attorney you know – and I sincerely hope it isn't – it's important to know that help is at hand.

I'm blessed that the state I live and practice in – Florida – is very progressive on this front. In fact, the Florida Supreme Court mandated that a program be created to identify and offer assistance to Bar members who suffer from substance abuse, mental health, or other disorders which negatively affect their lives and careers (Bar Rule 2-9.11).

Additionally, in 1986 the Florida Lawyers Assistance (FLA) program was created. FLA is funded by the Florida Bar, but is a separate and independent organization. There are over 30 support meetings and 400 volunteers around the State to help attorneys with substance abuse and psychological problems.

It's vital that you realize that Florida Lawyers Assistance is a confidential program. Confidentiality in voluntary cases is protected by a written agreement with The Florida Bar and the Bar guarantees the confidentiality of FLA records. See Bar Rule 3-7.1(j), Chap. 397.482-486, F.S. Judges, attorneys, law students, and support personnel who seek the assistance of FLA need not worry that FLA will report them to the Bar, the Board of Bar Examiners, or their employer. FLA's primary purpose is to assist the impaired attorney in their recovery.

While this precise level of support might not be available in the state in which you practice, I guarantee there is help for you out there. If you're having problems with a substance or compulsive behavior, please seek that help.

PERSISTENCE

One last thought I wanted to share with you. Good lawyers are persistent. Great lawyers don't just do the same thing over and over. They keep the same goal and when one approach fails, they try another.

So get prepared, put your eye on the horizon and move forward with confidence. Stay balanced and don't be afraid of failure. Persist in your efforts to be the best lawyer you can be.

SECTION II:
OUTSIDE

INTRODUCTION

Thomas Jefferson may have said it best: "In matters of style, swim with the current; in matters of principal, stand like a rock."

In more current times – meaning right now - the Middle District of Florida tells potential jurors, "No ripped/stained jeans, shorts, flip flops, tank tops or beach attire are allowed." But as a trip to the courthouse will tell you, a little more direction is needed for some folks.

That begs the question: What should you wear to court?

Honestly, I am not the person to tell you if you should wear pleated pants or how wide your tie should be. And I am the *last* person to opine on the proper skirt length or heel height. Those trends come and go, and I've reached a point in life where chasing trends just seems to make me look desperate.
But here's what I *can* do: legal and scientific research around this topic. As you'll see as Part Two of this book unfolds, it's possible to gather the academic literature on sartorial symbols to see if there is anything we, as attorneys or litigants (or just humans), can do to improve our chances of success at the courthouse or in life. All recommendations herein are not style tips, but are facts supported by the science in the footnotes.

In litigation there is no substitute for putting in the work, doing the legal research and having the facts on your side. Substance always wins over style.

But the simple reality is that how you look and present in the courtroom and the office is going to affect your outcome. That's not just an opinion, that is a fact borne out by scientific testing. We - lawyers, litigants, judges, jurors and citizens - are all preconditioned by our environment, and clothing is a big part of that environment.

So again, what should you wear to court? The short, easy answer is a dark blue suit, white shirt/blouse, a conservative tie or light jewelry, and the best business shoe in your budget. But if you'd like a deeper study to find out why this is the case, let's take a look at what the science tells us.

Chapter 1 ———————————————————————————————

THE IMPACT

What you wear is how you present yourself to the world, especially today, when human contacts are so quick. Fashion is instant language.

- Miuccia Prada

FIRST IMPRESSIONS MATTER

I think of my physical appearance as my first exhibit. I want to make sure I put forth to the judge or jury a presentation that is focused and credible. Part of that presentation is going to happen before I open my mouth. If I'm speaking to a jury, they're going to size me up before I start talking. If I arrive late to the courthouse, unshaven and wearing a wrinkled dress shirt, one of my goals is defeated before I even take my seat at counsel table.

You can dress to win. This is a phenomenon known as "sartorial manipulation," and it can literally make you a better negotiator and litigator. Researchers dressed test subjects in a variety of clothing - from tracksuits to business suits - and had them engage in negotiations with another subject unaware of the wardrobe manipulation. Not surprisingly, wearing a business suit facilitated greater profits and concessions than sweatpants. Wearing a business suit also increased testosterone levels in the male subjects.

So, simply wearing a business suit to a mediation may induce dominance and produce a better outcome for lawyers and their clients. And certainly sweatpants are to be avoided.[1]

The good news is we make a new first impression every day. There is no reason why you can't start projecting a more positive image today. And that image may have a greater impact than you think.

CLOTHES CAN MAKE OTHERS THINK YOU'RE SMARTER

Tracy Morris, a professor of psychology at West Virginia University, studied how attire impacts perception. For one test, Morris asked a group of professors to dress in three types of garb — formal professional (full dark suits), business casual (slacks or skirts and nice shirts), or casual (jeans, a plaid flannel, sneakers). The professors then gave lectures. Controlling for content, as well as non-verbal behavior, she then asked students to rate professors on several attributes involving competence, character, sociability, composure, and extroversion.

What she found: Perceptions of professional attributes, like competence, composure, and knowledge, "are effected most by dress, with formal dress resulting in the most positive perception." Perceptions of instructor competence were highest for those in the formal clothing, with business casual a close second. Not surprisingly, the lowest ratings were reserved for those in casual wear.

It's worth defining "formal professional" for the courtroom and dressing accordingly. The idea is not to show up at the courthouse or at work dressed for a gala. The idea is simply, if you're dressing like a schlub at the courthouse or your office, step it up a notch if you want others to see you as knowledgeable and firmly on top of your game.

DRESS ALSO AFFECTS HOW YOU SEE YOURSELF ON THE JOB

This next study is directed at those who are wearing jeans and sneakers in a mostly slacks and oxfords office. In other words, those who tend to dress more casually than their peers and other work colleagues. Even if you're not violating a dress code, some evidence says dressing "properly" has an impact on how you see your own skill set.

In a 1994 study, North Illinois University's Yoon-Hee Kwon studied how clothing impacts the way you rate yourself on ten occupational attributes: Responsibility, competence, knowledgeability, professionalism, honesty, reliability, intelligence, trustworthiness, willingness to work hard, and efficiency. (All key components of professionalism, by the way). When Kwon cross-referenced these attributes against broad guidelines like "properly dressed" or "not properly dressed," she found that when wearing appropriate clothes, a person's sense of these occupational traits in themselves was augmented.

In a separate study, participants were told to appear for the experiment in either formal or casual wear.
Upon arrival they were asked to describe themselves and their particular personality traits. Consistent with the study above, those dressed formally described themselves more formally and more quickly agreed with formal personality traits. Likewise, the casually dressed responded in the reverse.[2]

I would wager that most lawyers have one suit that makes them feel like they own the courtroom. And my guess is that it's dark blue. Bottom line, clothing is going to change how you feel in the courtroom and the office. A study examining workplace attire discovered that respondents felt most authoritative, trustworthy, and competent when wearing formal business attire but friendliest when wearing casual or business casual attire.[3]

Do you have a multiple day trial coming up? Would it help you during jury selection to feel a little friendlier? Perhaps wearing a sport coat or something a little less formal would help you get in a more conversational frame of mind. Then you can come back for the remainder of trial in that formal suit that makes you feel like the authority in the courtroom.

CLOTHES CAN ACTUALLY MAKE YOU SMARTER

Perhaps the most definitive article of clothing in the courtroom is the judge's black robe. In a 2017 survey of judges by the National Judicial College about robes, one judge responded, "I'm often reminded of the Wizard in Oz when I put it on. Even though it does not make me smarter, more compassionate or discerning, I feel that it does!"

Maybe we should give the robe more credit. Recent research suggests the black robe conceivably does make judges better at their job.

Lately, the phrase "enclothed cognition" has found its way into business school vocabulary. The term was coined by Adam D. Galinsky, a professor at Northwestern's Kellogg School of Management, who found that when people don a white lab coat they believe belongs to a doctor, they become more focused and careful, effectively a little smarter, when performing cognitive tasks. "Clothes invade the body and brain, putting the wearer into a different psychological state," said *The New York Times* about Galinsky's findings.

As a lawyer, abstract thinking can be an essential tool for solving our client's problems. Studies have shown that formal clothing increases your abstract cognitive processing. [4]

It is up to you whether you want your PJs, sweatpants or jeans invading your mind while you work, or something a little more smart and attractive. I'm not saying you should show up at your law office tomorrow in a white lab coat. But it's worth thinking about what symbolizes smart and effective in your own office and swim with that tide.

Chapter 2 ————————————————

THE BASICS

Fashion is a tool... to compete in life outside the home.
People like you better, without knowing why, because
people always react well to a person they like the looks of.

- Mary Quant

A gain, I am the last person to give full-on fashion tips. For me, it's easier to point out what *not* to wear to court. Here are a few basic ways for attorneys to feel prepared and comfortable in the courtroom.

1. Attend to personal grooming. Get a haircut, keep your nails trimmed, brush your teeth and don't be afraid of soap. Sometimes attorneys have to confer in ways that bring us in close contact. Bad breath or body odor is not the impression you want to make.

2. Go light on the jewelry. You will never make a mistake by wearing too little jewelry. Avoid anything that jingles or clanks on the table. (I like to wear cufflinks, but I don't at trial for this reason.) Jewelry should not be distracting.

3, Wear makeup, but not too much. Studies indicate that women who wear makeup are rated higher in trustworthiness and competence. However, testing showed the highest contrast makeup decreased judgments of trustworthiness.[5]

4. Make fit and comfort a priority. There is nothing that will make you feel more comfortable in the courtroom than a properly fitting suit. Spend some money on a good trial suit and a great tailor. Dr Karen Pine tested the perception of men wearing an off-the-rack suit vs. a custom tailored suit. The model wearing the tailored suit scored higher on all positive attributes. And for women, a suit with a skirt vs. a suit with trousers rated more favorably. [6]

5. Keep it clean. Make sure your shoes are shined to perfection and your clothing is pressed.

6. Forego making a fashion statement. Trial isn't the time to "express yourself" through your personal presentation. I have had more than one client become defensive when I've suggested tattoos be covered, facial hair be shaved and a fashion forward designer suit be exchanged for a more conservative color and cut. You should certainly be yourself at trial, but at the same time, you'll want the judge to focus on your testimony and the facts of your case with minimal distraction. Jurors don't know you; that first impression is critical.

DOES THE COLOR OF YOUR TIE MATTER?

For men, the most defining elements of their wardrobe are their ties. By its nature, the tie is front and center. They come in a wide variety of colors and patterns and can define the wearer at a glance. A collection of ties can likely tell how old you are, who you are and what image you are trying to project to the world. So, what color should you wear?

In the 2004 Olympic Games, competitors in tae kwon do, boxing and wrestling matches who wore red jerseys won more often than those wearing blue. Subsequent research in these sports showed that wearing red increased heart rate and strength in test participants.[7]

Of course this study prompted yet another study, this one of English football and whether the "colour" of jerseys affected the outcome. A matched-pairs analysis of red and non-red wearing teams in eight English cities shows significantly better performance of red teams over a 55-year period. These effects on long-term success confirm that wearing red enhances performance in a variety of competitive contexts.[8]

By now you're thinking, *I guess I should wear a red tie.*

But here's where it gets complicated. A test was done to gauge the perception of athletes wearing red, blue and green. The tests showed that athletes wearing red in boxing and wrestling were judged as more aggressive and more likely to win than athletes wearing blue or green. However, athletes wearing green were judged fairer in boxing and wrestling than athletes wearing red.

Clearly, the tie you wear carries specific meanings that affect others' judgments. But do you want to be seen as more likely to win, or do you want to be judged fairly?[9]

IS IT THE SHOES?

"Thin slicing" is the idea in psychology that we can find meaning and make inferences from minimal amounts of information. And there is probably no better predictive piece of clothing than the shoe. A good pair of shoes will immediately elevate your wardrobe, and a bad pair will sabotage a first impression faster than anything else you wear.

You can tell a lot about a person solely based on their shoes. In a University of Kansas study participants were successfully able to predict age, gender, income, and attachment anxiety of shoe owners based solely on pictures of their favorite shoes.[10]

Shoes are the one piece of clothing that change the wearer physically. By adjusting your height and stance, shoes put you in a physically different position and affect your psychological position as well.

Shoes are also the piece of clothing that can make you most uncomfortable. Poor fitting or poorly made shoes make you uncomfortable, and when you're uncomfortable it shows. You fidget, you walk funny, you're distracted, you frequently switch positions when standing, and you give non-verbal signals that others pick up. Unfortunately, these are the same signals that liars put out. How is a jury to know if you're lying or merely wearing uncomfortable shoes?

The net-net: buy the best pair of shoes you can afford, and make sure they fit you properly. Keep them polished and in good condition. It will send the right message to everyone in the court.

PULL IT ALL TOGETHER

Plan your wardrobe and budget accordingly. Start with a basic blue suit, five white dress shirts or blouses, and two or three pairs of good shoes. Then build from there. Be patient and shop the sales. Another tip: Most major department stores offer professional shopping help for no additional cost. By starting a relationship with a member of the sales staff, you'll be alerted first about new merchandise, as well as upcoming sales and store events.

Chapter 3 ———————————————————————

THE NEXT LEVEL

Don't be into trends. Don't make fashion own you, but you decide what you are, what you want to express by the way you dress and the way you live.

- Gianni Versace

KNOW YOUR AUDIENCE AND ENVIRONMENT

John Molloy in *New Dress for Success* said, "[T]he message that is most likely to get you into trouble is that you think of yourself as a superior being from a more sophisticated company, town or country, and you wear clothing that loudly announces that fact."

Your choice of clothing is going to talk before you do. A first impression is going to happen before you open your mouth. Humans had to evaluate other humans before there was language, and we're wired to quickly judge others based on appearance and circumstances. Dressing consistent with local dress codes will keep you out of trouble.

Researchers found that people who value uniqueness will rate the status and competence of a speaker higher if he wears red Converse shoes while lecturing. This increased rating suggests that wearing something a little bit outside of the norm is an indication of power and the wearer has a confidence to risk the social costs of such behaviors.[11]

While I would never recommend red Converse in the courtroom, a bright tie or scarf may be a signal, to the right audience, of your confidence in your position and a sign that you know what you are doing. Be careful though, as the positive inference disappears when the observer is unfamiliar with the environment. So a judge who is in the courtroom every day may appreciate your jaunty pocket square but a juror, new to the courthouse, may not see it the same way.

I once overheard a prosecutor and public defender talking about how brightly colored shoes (blue and orange respectively) made them feel more assertive. However, they both agreed that said shoes may be fine for a routine calendar call with the judge, but they would *not* be appropriate in front of a jury.

THE CASE FOR WEARING A UNIFORM

J. Wayne Reitz, former president of the University of Florida, always wore a blue suit. Nobody knew if he owned one suit or ten, but that's how he showed up to work everyday.

Taking a cue from Reitz, there is rarely a time or place during work hours that showing up in a blue suit will be seen as inappropriate.

There is also a value in removing the decision of what to wear from your morning routine. As lawyers we have to make a multitude of important decisions each day. Taking the small, mundane decisions out of the day gives us more energy and focus for our work. Einstein bought several grey suits because he didn't want to waste his brainpower on clothing. And I know I'm not Einstein and need all the brainpower I can harness!

I don't think you need to throw out all your clothes as you work your way toward your version of a uniform, but think about simplifying your wardrobe and how it could impact your morning preparations.

EVEN YOUR "OFF THE CLOCK" LOOK NEEDS MANAGEMENT

Justice Cardozo said, "Membership in the bar is a privilege burdened with conditions. A fair and professional character is one of them." Character is how we behave 24/7. Character is how we behave when no one is looking, but people's perception of our character is based on what they see. The Bar rules are in place all day and all night, and our after-hours dress and conduct has an impact on our work hours.

Consistency in your behavior, on and off the clock, will be recognized. (And inconsistency may also be recognized.) Your actions in the real world and online should reflect a "fair and professional character." This includes how you dress when not at work. This doesn't mean you need to show up to a pool party dressed like you're going to the courthouse. But it does mean that your choice of swimsuit deserves some consideration just like your trial suit.

CONSISTENCY HELPS IN PERSONAL BRANDING

When you think of Steve Jobs you get a vision of him in his signature black turtleneck. Mark Zuckerberg used a T-shirt and hoodie to define and set himself apart. Adopting a consistent look can help in your personal branding. As a lawyer, you won't get away with turtlenecks or hoodies, but a consistent, professional dress can help to establish you, in the minds of Judges and colleagues, as a person who can be trusted and respected.

Think of a lawyer in your community, in your field, that you respect and admire. Odds are you're picturing them dressed professionally. Think of the lawyers that you refer cases to outside of your practice area. We only refer to attorneys that we know have a professional appearance and are competent.

So the advice for lawyers is to dress for the cases you *want*, not the cases you *have*. The right clothing is going to affect how others see you, how you feel about yourself, and how you actually perform.

THE VALUE OF MODESTY

Anyone with a teenage daughter will tell you that modesty is an underappreciated value. And in today's social media world, modesty is a value that has a hard time finding traction in any form. Modest lawyers almost never become famous.

But modesty in your clothing can be an asset. I would wager that one of the things that is common across all of the respected attorneys in your area is they are modest in their clothing. There is nothing flashy about the way they present themselves. And they are never – ever - disheveled.

Your clothing should not distract from your message. As discussed in the studies above, your choice of clothing is going to talk before you do. A first impression is going to happen before you open your mouth. Humans had to evaluate other humans before there was language and we are quick to judge others based on appearance and circumstances. Thus, dressing with modesty can help others focus on your arguments and what you have to say.

Research has shown that clothing style and gender influenced subjects' perceptions of others. In particular, subjects rated others wearing similar clothing as themselves more positively, and that the ratings of women were less harsh then those of men.[12]

A majority of men in the United States only own one suit. And since they only own one suit, it is usually a conservative dark blue suit that can be worn to funerals and weddings.

Dressing in a modest style, similar to what a juror himself wears, may cause them to view you more positively.

PHYSICAL FITNESS COUNTS

In addition to being able to choose our clothing, we can also choose our level of fitness. Your physical appearance and fitness affects how others perceive you. And while I don't necessarily believe that the amount of money you make is an indication of your level of professionalism, income is a useful measuring stick for evaluating the value of personal appearance.

If you've won the genetic lottery and are tall and/or attractive, studies have shown you are going to earn more. But more importantly (because we can control it), your fitness level will also affect your earning potential. Researchers have correlated working out and income. The scientific realities are that obese workers get paid less, and that employees who work out regularly (three times a week) get paid more.[13]

ONE LAST THOUGHT

Mark Twain said, "Clothes make the man. Naked people have little or no influence on society." However, I do not believe that "clothes make the man" (or woman). But what we wear does influence our perception of each other and the way we see ourselves. With this research, I hope I've opened your mind to the many ways you can control not only the way others perceive you, but also the way you perceive yourself. So many aspects of our appearance can be shaped for maximum impact in court and in life. Why not seize those opportunities?

SECTION III:
WHAT NOT TO WEAR TO COURT

INTRODUCTION

In difficult times fashion is always outrageous.

- Elsa Schiaparelli

I would like to finish by confessing to you that I have a bad habit. I know when I go to the courthouse it is for serious business, my client is accused of a crime or has a claim to bring. I am prepared and focused like a laser on the matter at hand.

And then, walking through the courthouse halls something will catch my eye and I get distracted for a moment. Someone will draw my attention with what they chose to wear to the courthouse that day. And I think to myself, "That person got out of bed this morning, knowing they were coming to the courthouse, to stand in front of a judge (for their own serious business) and this is what they deliberately decided to wear!"

And what do I do? Take a picture, of course. #WhatNotToWearToCourt

Now, I do have a set of rules that I follow. Perhaps these rules are better referred to as guidelines, as I do break them every now and then.

First, I don't take pictures of simply bad fashion choices. That would be too easy. The criminal courthouse is full of people who have made poor decisions and bad fashion is the least of their problems. I limit my pictures to people coming to court to make a statement. Today's t-shirts offer people a broad canvas to testify and give witness before they even open their mouth.

Second, I ask permission. Only one person to date has declined my request for a photo. Like I said, most people I photograph are there to make a statement and are more than happy to pose for me. Occasionally, I will just snap a picture on the run, but usually I ask first.

Third, I don't take pictures in the courtroom. I may bend this one if the judge is not on the bench. Usually I just catch people in the hallway outside the courtroom.

And lastly, I don't post a picture for the purpose of making fun of someone. #WhatNotToWearToCourt is not intended to humiliate anyone or mock anyone. Except for lawyers without socks, those guys are fair game.

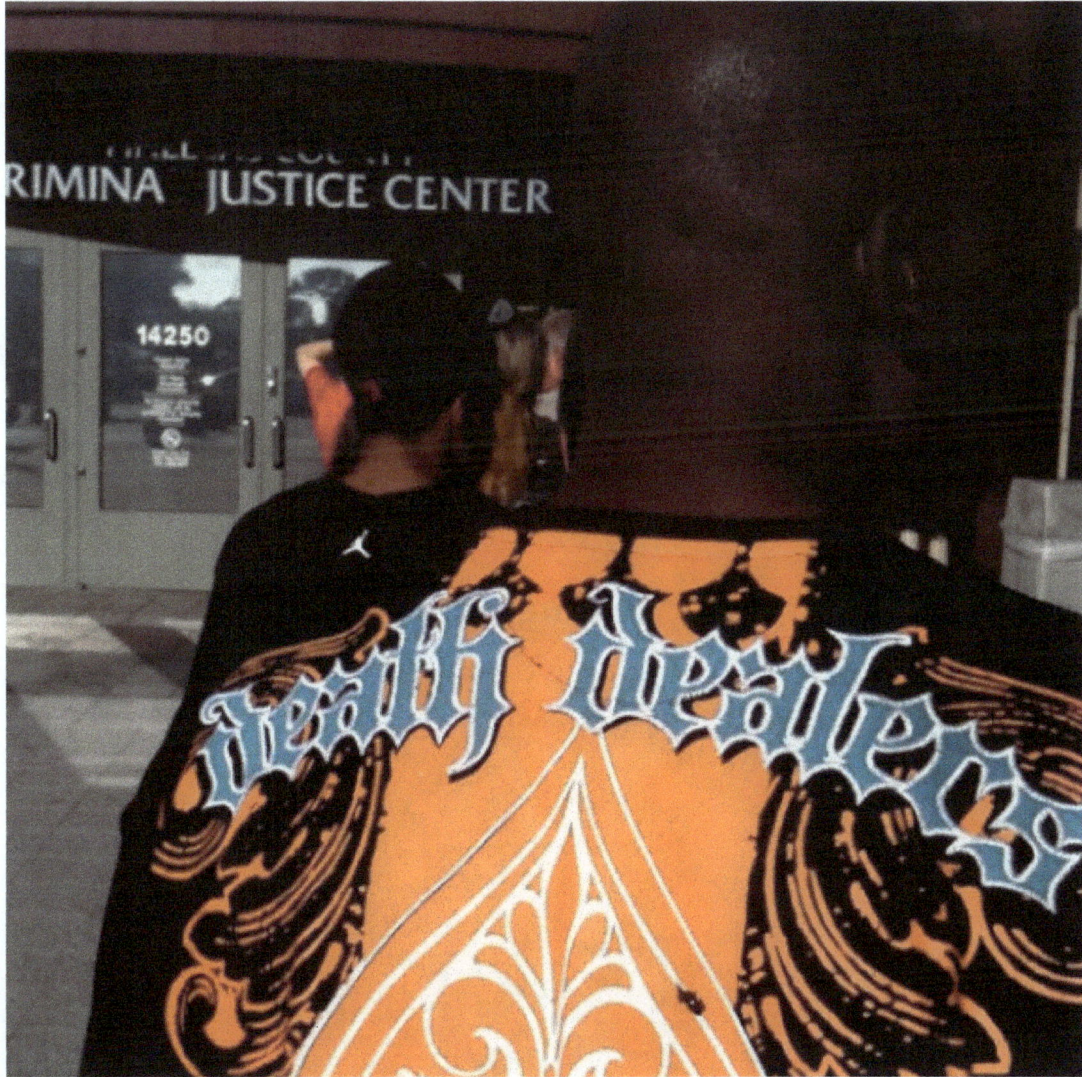

The shot that started it all.

LAWYERS, GUNS AND MONEY

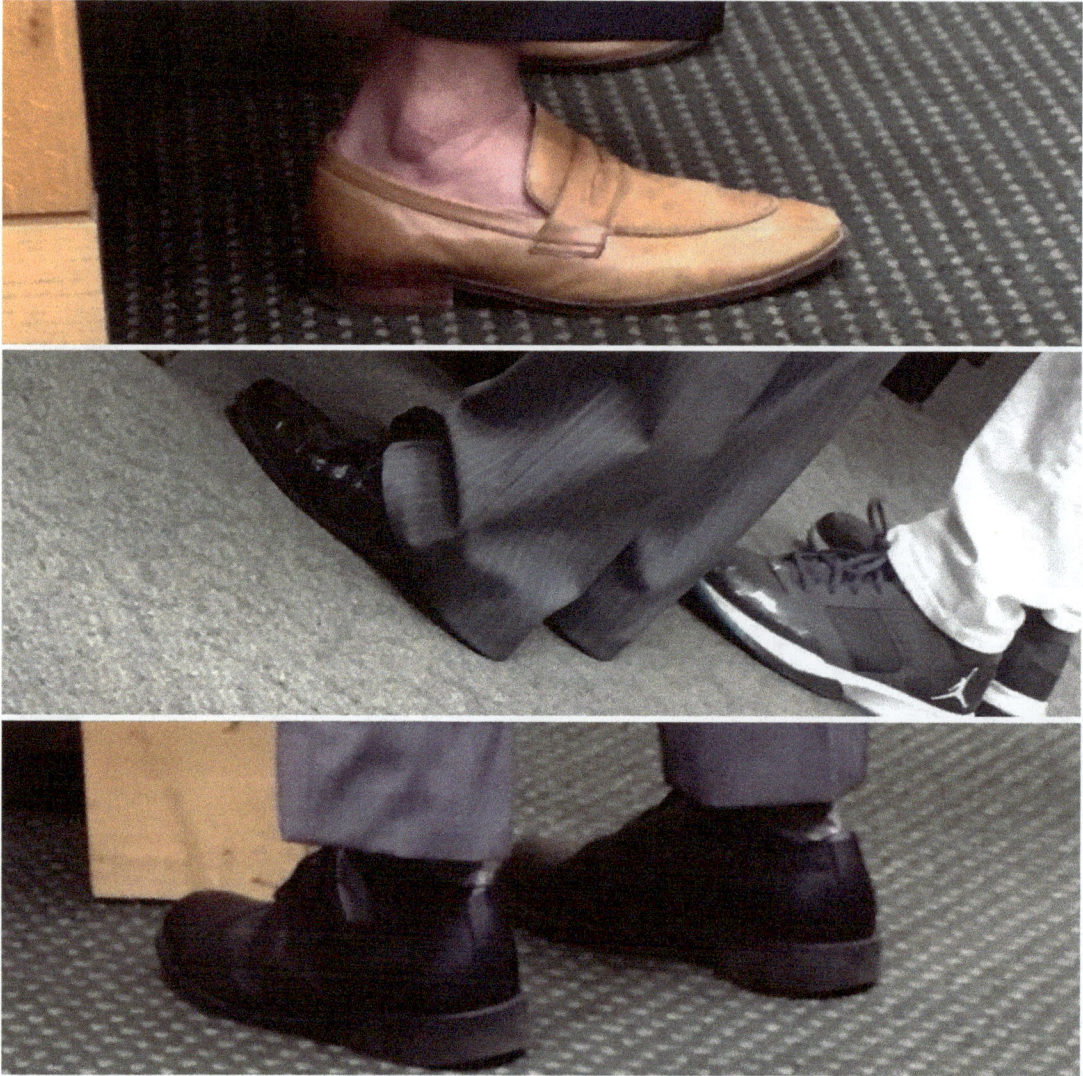

See Outside, Chapter 2
on proper tailoring.

Socks that cover your calves.
They're not just for baseball players.

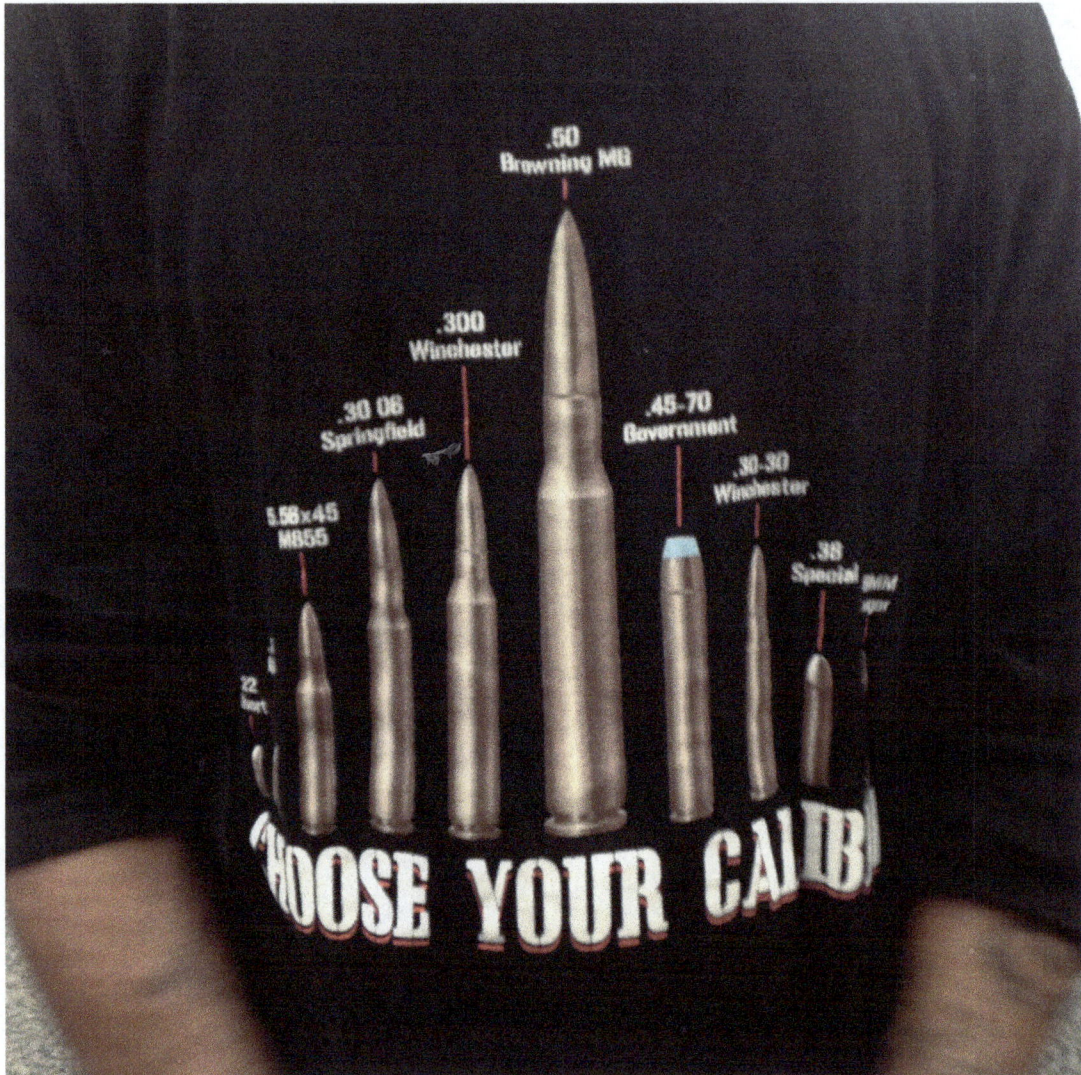

Decisions, Decisions, Decisions

When you care enough
to send your very best.

Good to let the judge know
you have priorities.

Self Made Self Paid

FOUR STAGES OF COURTHOUSE GRIEF

Denial

More Denial

Bargaining

Acceptance

A MESSAGE TO
THE JUDGE

You'll have to speak up, Judge.

15 yard penalty for taunting.

But it is so worth it!

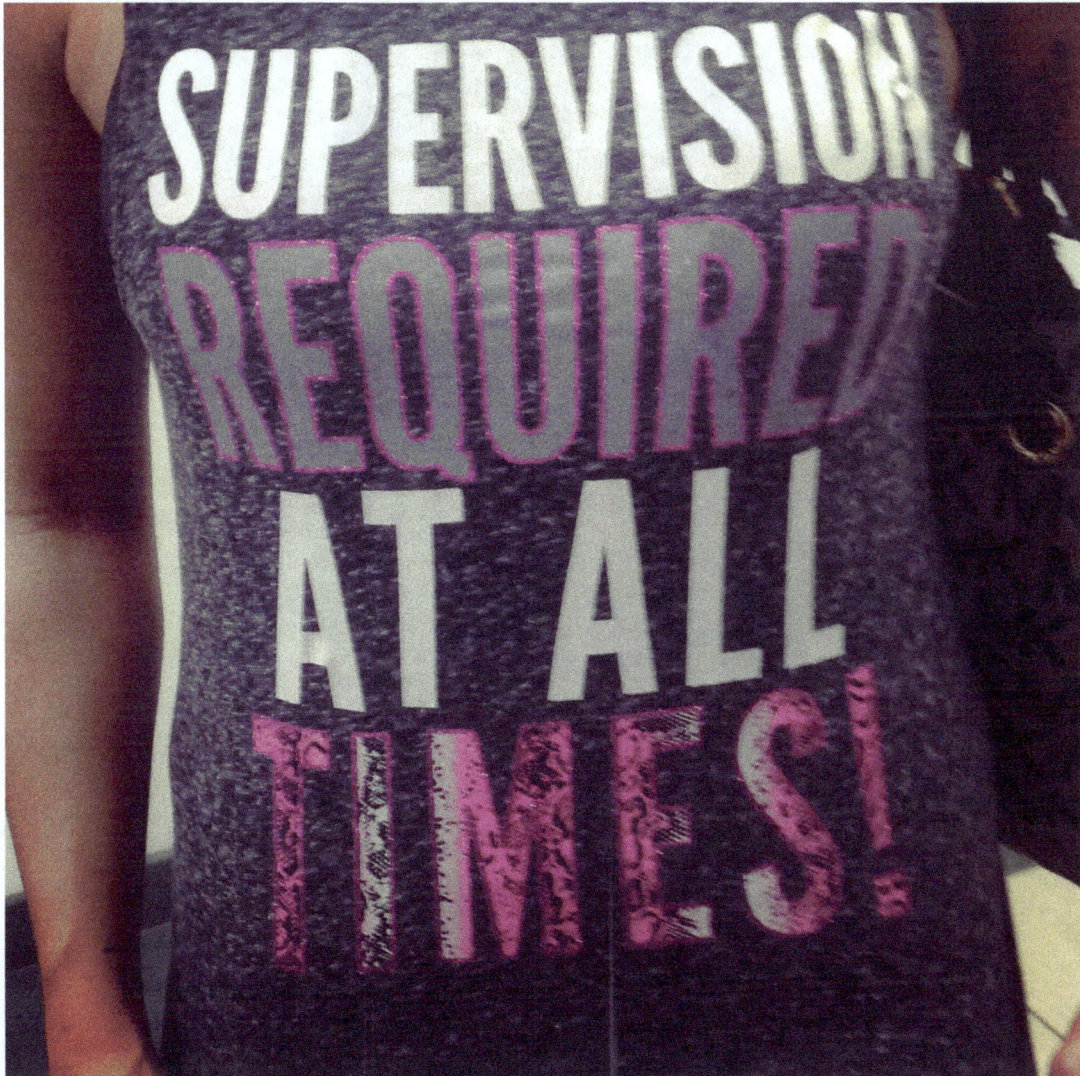

Poor probation candidate.

Hey Judge, can you do me a favor?

PAIRS

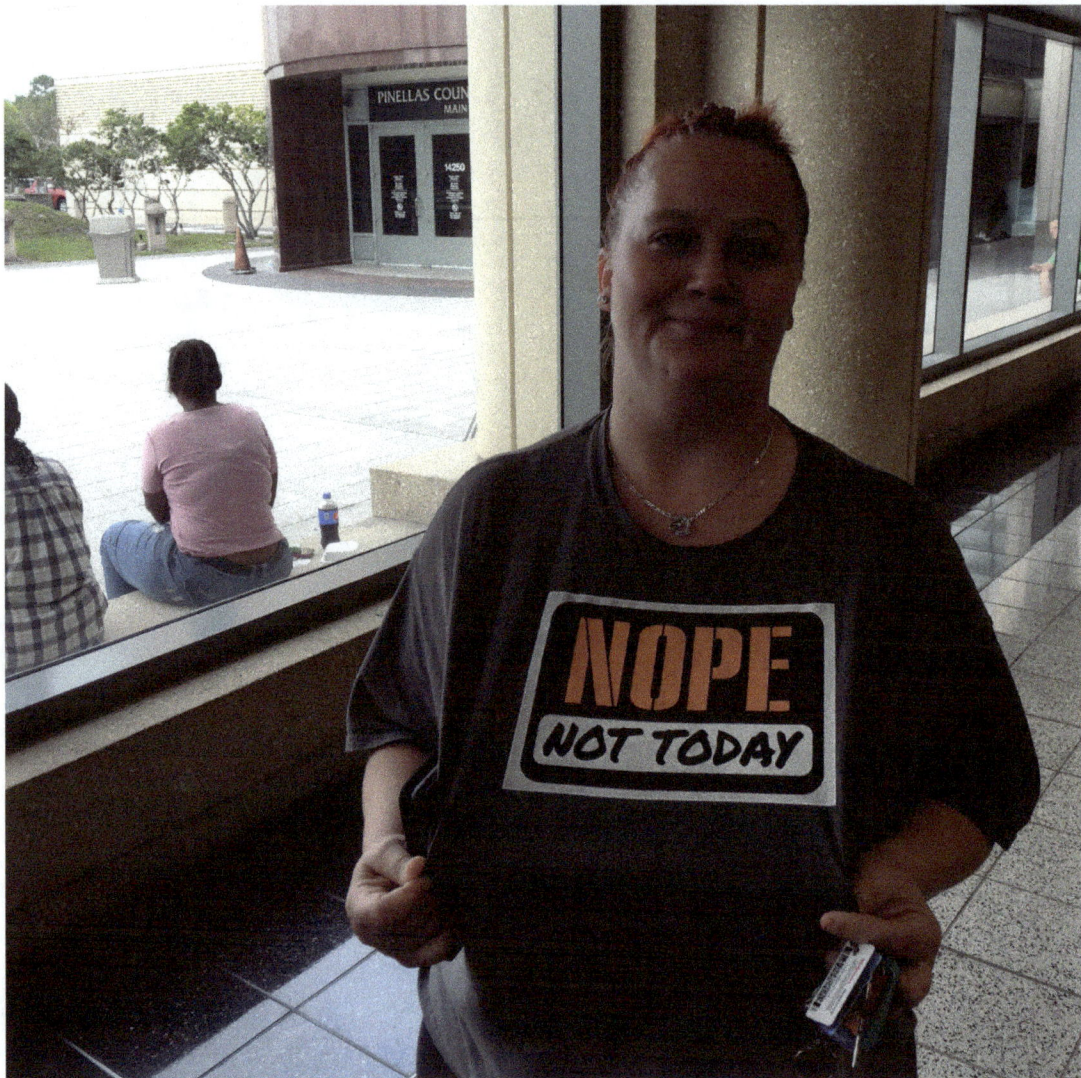

In case you come across an Orgasm
Donor at the courthouse.

Nope. Not Today.

Maybe he should have been.

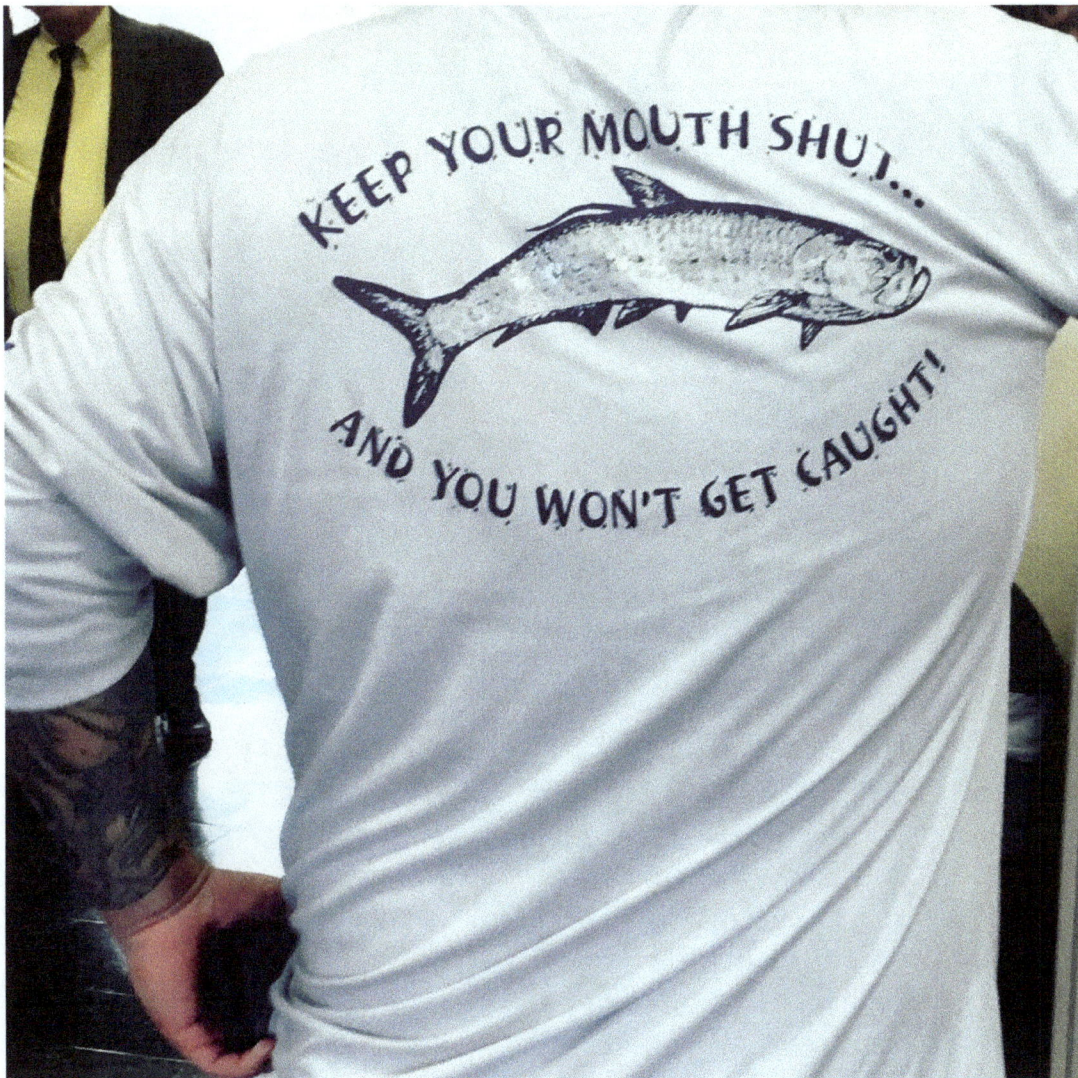

Good advice for everyone at the
criminal courthouse.

B YOUR SELF or C YOUR SELF would
be better choices.

I Fd Up.

"IT" being a Youthful
Offender sentence.

Young and Wild

Bring in the jury.

I'll take the first six.

Malt Liquor and Mary Jane

Manson and Midriff

This could work, if the judge raises Saxon Pigeons.
See Inside, Chapter 1 on knowing the judge.

Jeans in court are questionable. Acid washed
is never a good choice. And elastic cuffs???

See Outside, Chapter 2 on keeping it clean.

Like this guy.

DRUG COURT

Thank you for your service.

Nike shirts take on a new meaning at
the courthouse. #JustDoIt

Weed Hat

It's a shame the font can't be bigger.

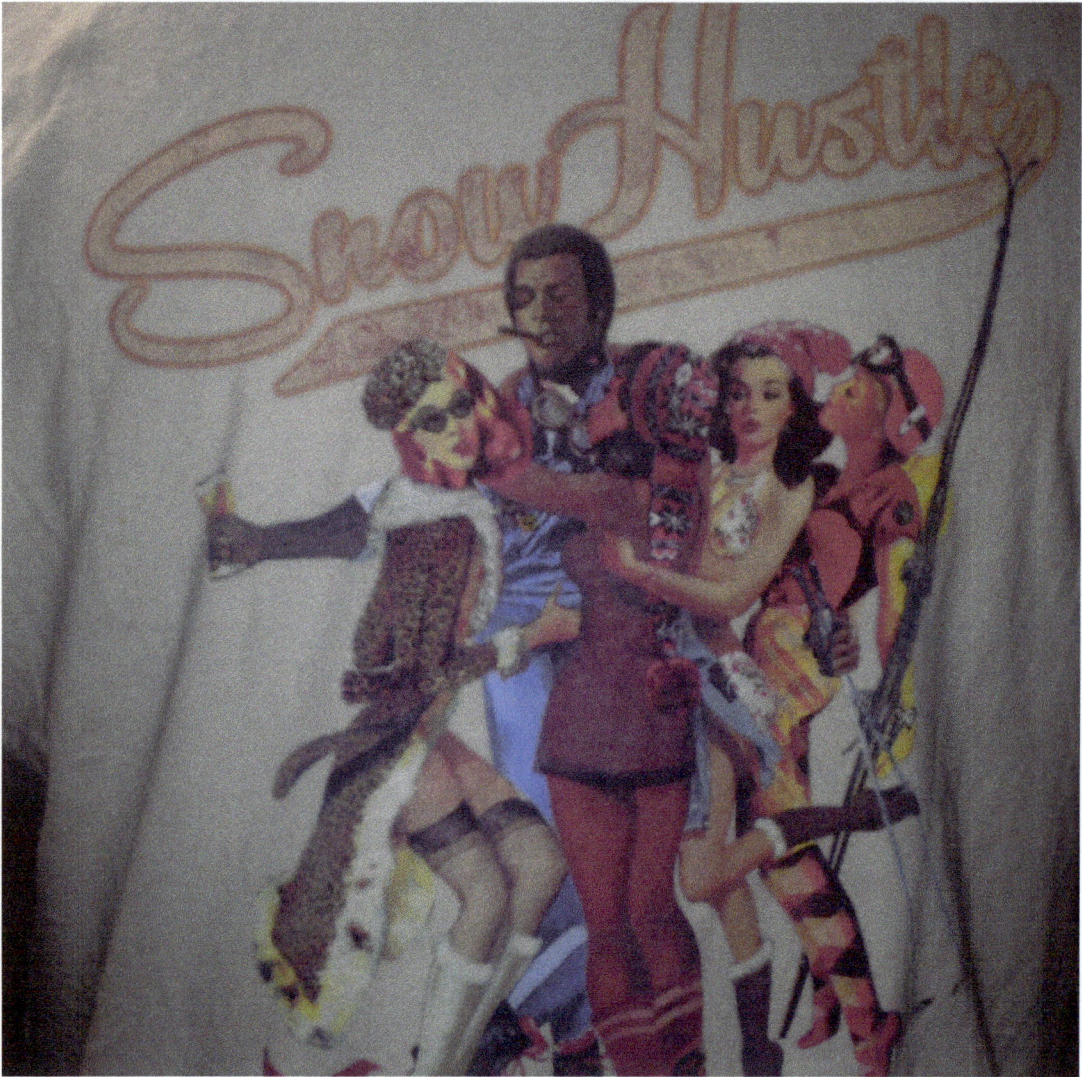

Who knew Bogota had skiing?

User Friendly

Not a role model. #ecstacy

AS SEEN AT THE COURTHOUSE

Let's get ready to rumble!

Brunch. It's the most
important meal of the day.

Stickmen can't high-five.
Technically, it's a high-one.

There are easier ways to
get out of jury duty.

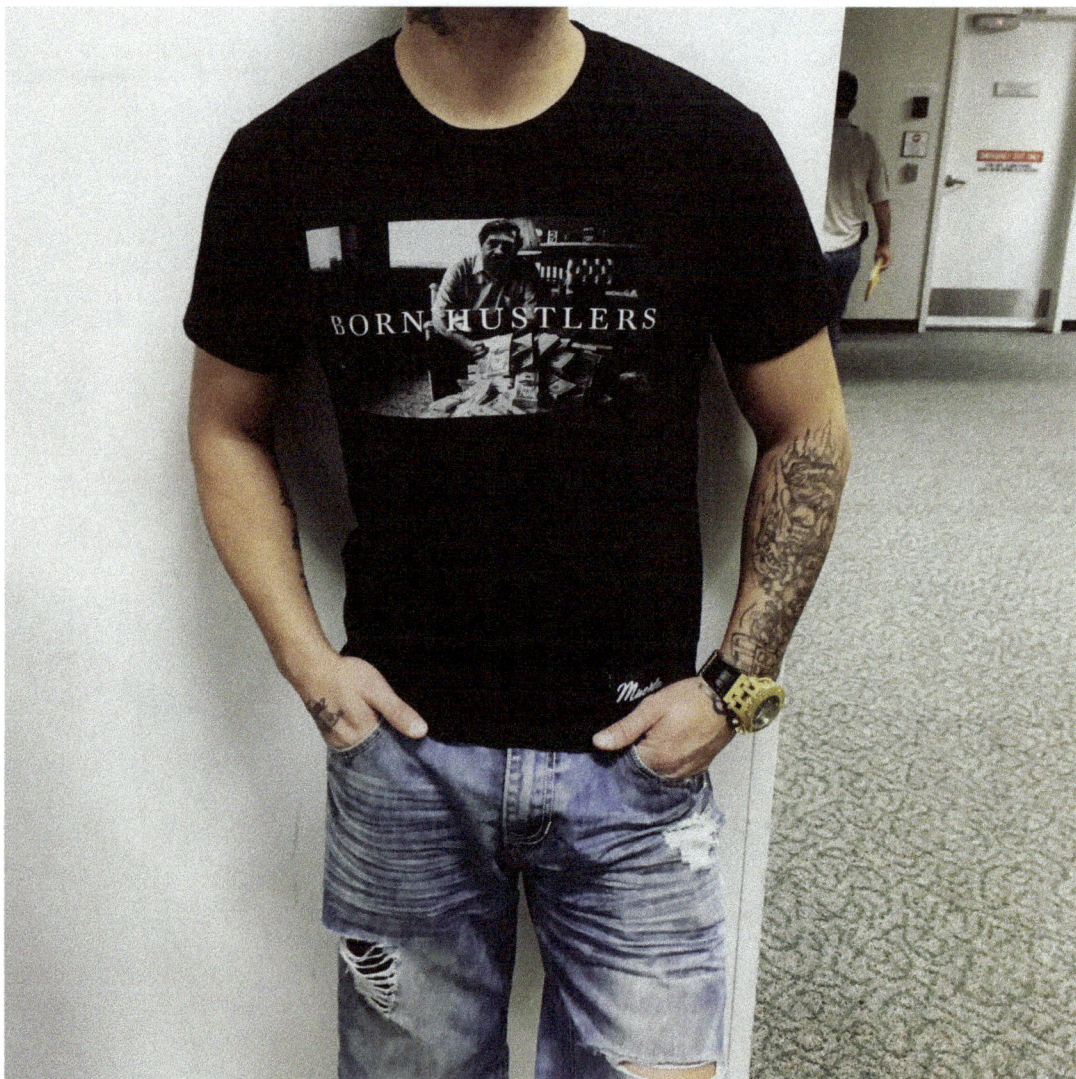

The Pablo Escobar tshirt is the
new Scarface shirt.

Even Pixar isn't safe.

Probably best to leave your
hobbies at home.

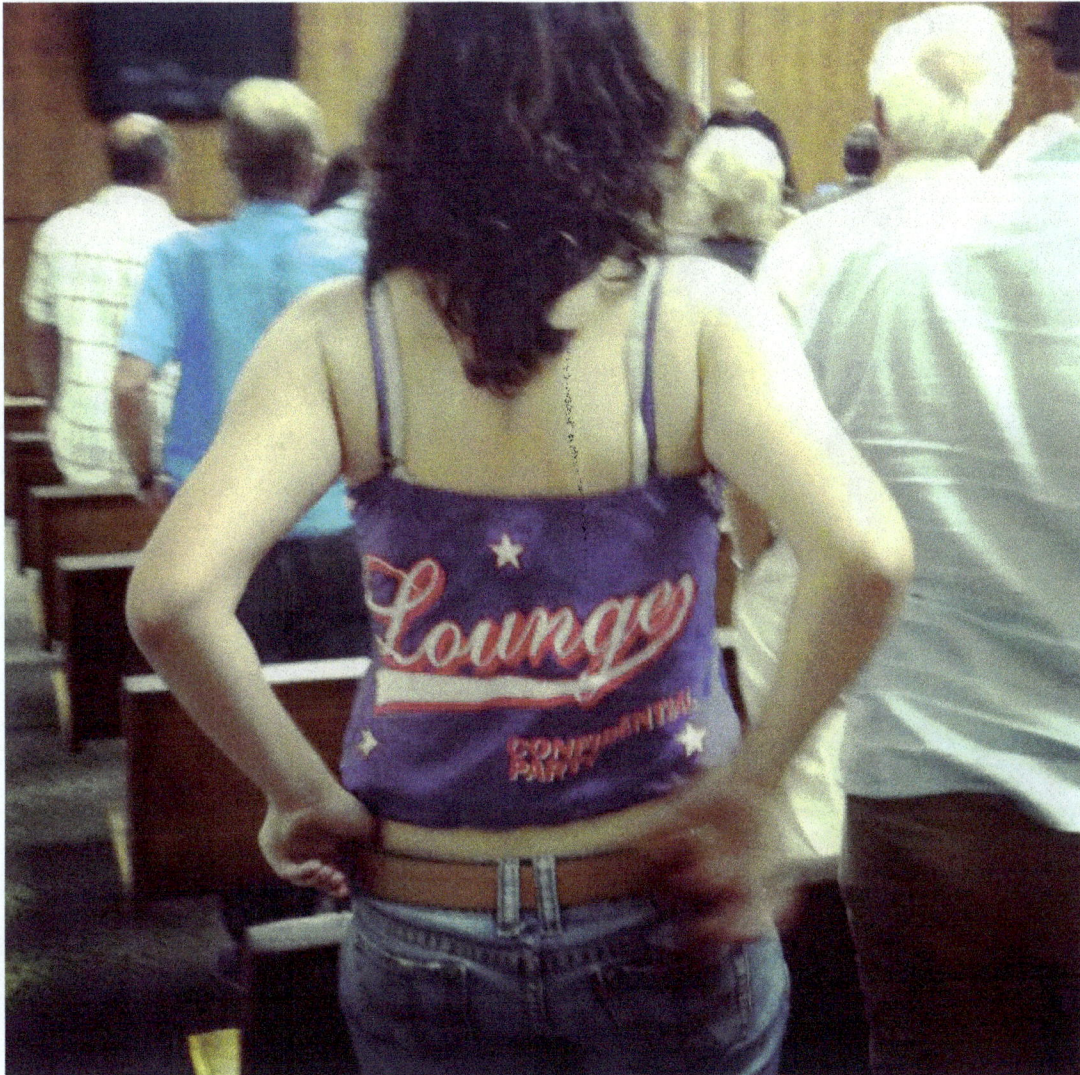

The picture does not capture
the silkiness of this top.

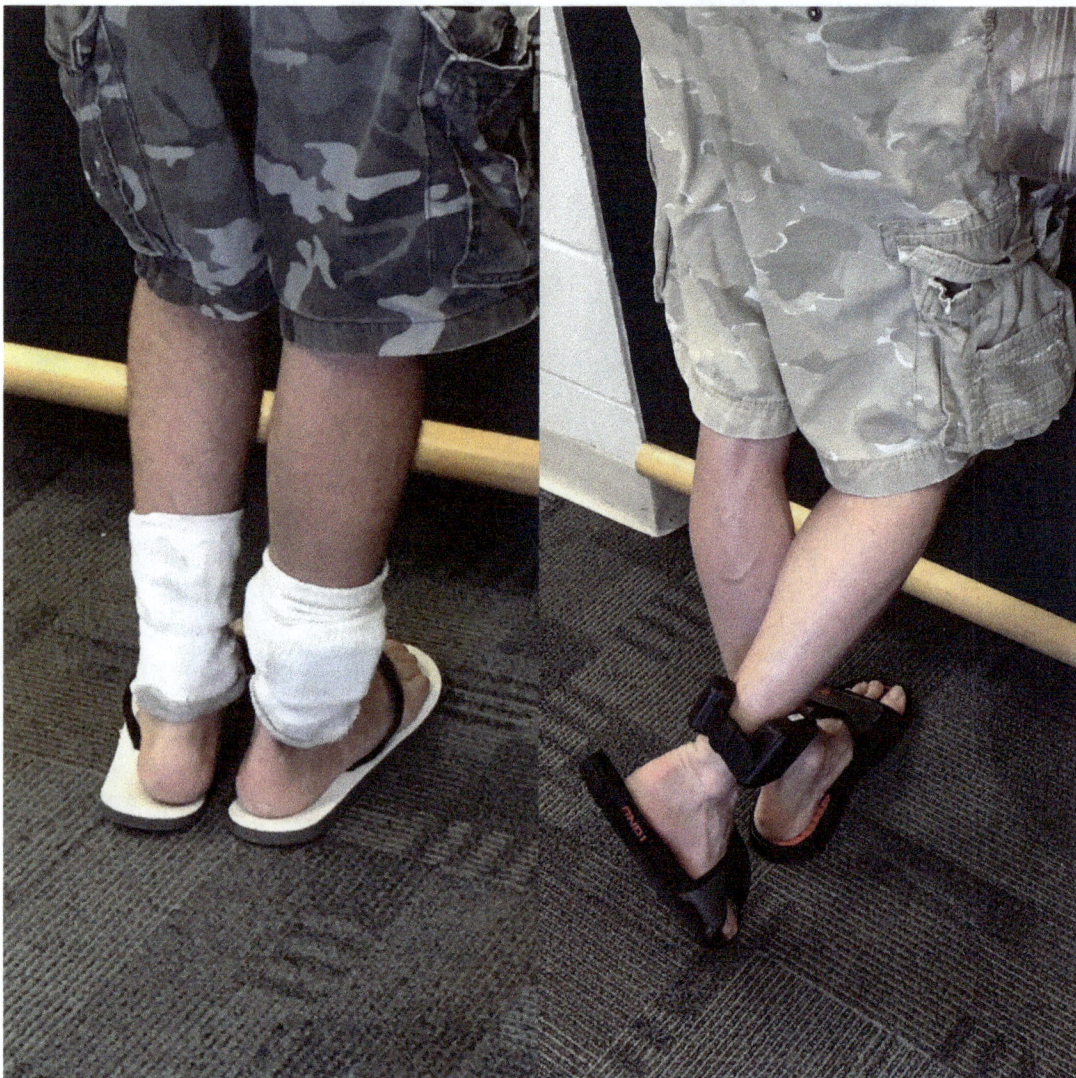

Some do camo better
than others.

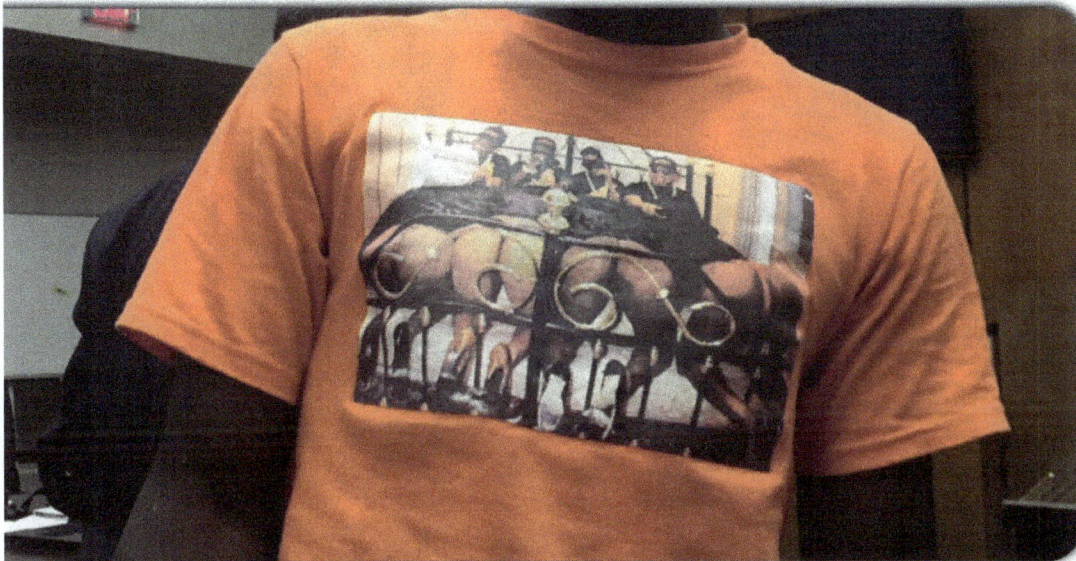

No 2 Live Crew tour shirt is
appropriate for court. #saynotocrack

Work It

■ ACKNOWLEDGEMENTS

The genesis of this book was not lawyering, but paddling.

A few years back I had the idea to take people who were in recovery from addiction out for a stand up paddleboard lesson. My friend Brody Welte brought out some Yoloboards and that outing with Footsteps Recovery eventually grew into the nonprofit, Paddle Addict. Bert Savage helped me incorporate and Gary Hallas assisted in putting on some paddle events to fund the organization. Getting folks in recovery on a paddleboard, on the water, exercising and having fun sober was a great expansion of what I was doing professionally and I wanted to do more.

Eventually I recognized that the lessons of balance, forward movement and getting back on when you fall off are lessons lawyers need as well, and I expanded the concepts of Paddle Addict to professionals. This book is an encapsulation of these ideas.

I appreciate the help of Jon LaBudde, Christian Cook, The Pinellas Association of Women Lawyers and everyone who has come out and paddled with me as I developed and refined the lessons in this book.

Through it all my wife has been a huge support and I could not have done any of this without her toleration of my trials and errors.

The book itself would not be readable without the gracious help of Dana Wood and I appreciate her talents.

I leaned on the help of Mike Sexton for some of the captions in Chapter 3. The better ones were not suitable for print. Maybe we can use them in the next book.

Thanks to my mom and dad who never gave up on me even in years of some very questionable fashion choices (and other poor choices as well).

I am grateful for the help of Martin, Jeff and the staff at Kirby's Mens Wear for their assistance in dressing me consistent with the ideas in this book. I encourage everyone to seek out a good store with a great tailor.

I also wanted to express my gratitude to the judges of the Sixth Circuit, especially Judge Campbell, Judge Coleman and Judge Burgess for their encouragement. Their focus on professionalism is an inspiration to us all.

∎NOTES ────────────────────

1 Sartorial symbols of social class elicit class-consistent behavioral and physiological responses: A dyadic approach. Kraus, Michael W.; Mendes, Wendy Berry, Journal of Experimental Psychology: General, Vol 143(6), Dec 2014, 2330-2340.]

2 "The Clothing Makes the Self" Via Knowledge Activation, B Hannover, U Kühnen - Journal of Applied Social Psychology, 2002

3 Peluchette, J. V. and Karl, K. (2007), The impact of workplace attire on employee self-perceptions. Human Resource Development Quarterly, 18: 345–360. doi:10.1002/hrdq.1208

4 Slepian, Michael L., et al. "The cognitive consequences of formal clothing." Social Psychological and Personality Science 6.6 (2015): 661-668.

5 Etcoff NL, Stock S, Haley LE, Vickery SA, House DM (2011) Cosmetics as a Feature of the Extended Human Phenotype: Modulation of the Perception of Biologically Important Facial Signals. PLoS ONE 6(10): e25656.

6 The Effect of Appearance on First Impressions, Professor Karen J Pine, Professor Ben Fletcher & Neil Howlett, University of Hertfordshire

7 Sport Exerc Psychol. 2013 Feb;35(1):44-9. Influence of red jersey color on physical parameters in combat sports., Dreiskaemper D1, Strauss B, Hagemann N, Büsch D.

8 J Sports Sci. 2008 Apr;26(6):577-82. doi: 10.1080/02640410701736244. Red shirt colour is associated with long-term team success in English football. Attrill MJ, Gresty KA, Hill RA, Barton RA.

9 J Sport Exerc Psychol. 2015 Apr;37(2):207-12. doi: 10.1123/jsep.2014-0274. The effect of uniform color on judging athletes' aggressiveness, fairness, and chance of winning. Krenn B

10 Gillath, O., Bahns, A. J., Ge, F., & Crandall, C. S. (2012). Shoes as a source of first impressions. Journal of Research in Personality, 46, 423-430.

11 Bellezza, Silvia, Francesca Gino, and Anat Keinan. "The Red Sneakers Effect: Inferring Status and Competence from Signals of Nonconformity." Journal of Consumer Research 41, no. 1 (June 2014): 35–54.

12 Reid A., Lancuba V., Morrow B. (1997). Clothing style and formation of first impressions. Perceptual and Motor Skills, 84, 237–238.

13 "Gender and Race Wage Gaps Attributable to Obesity" by Avi Dor PhD, Christine Ferguson JD, Ellen Tan PhDc, Lucas Divine, and Jo Palmer. November 17, 2011. The George Washington University School of Public Health and Health Services, and Kosteas, Vasilios D. "Effect of Exercise on Earnings: Evidence from the NLSY." Working Paper, Department of Economics, Cleveland State University, September 20, 2010.

ABOUT
THE AUTHOR

Bruce Denson is a lawyer, speaker and writer. His legal practice consists mainly of representing people against the government in criminal matters and against tobacco companies for the harm cigarettes have ravaged on society. He founded and operates Paddle Addict, Inc., a non-profit helping people with addiction issues through water sport activities. He is committed to the idea that we can all do better and everyone deserves a second chance.

Bruce@TheDensonFirm.com

www.TheDensonFirm.com

On Twitter @**brucedenson**
On Instagram @**brucedenson**
On Facebook at **www.facebook.com/TheDensonFirm/**